United States Government Accountability Office

Testimony

Before the Committee on Oversight and Government Reform, House of Representatives

For Release on Delivery
Expected at 9:30 a.m. EDT
Wednesday, July 10, 2013

FINANCIAL AND PERFORMANCE MANAGEMENT

I0448699

More Reliable and Complete Information Needed to Address Federal Management and Fiscal Challenges

Statement of Gene L. Dodaro
Comptroller General of the United States

GAO-13-752T

Highlights of GAO-13-752T, a testimony before the Committee on Oversight and Government Reform, House of Representatives

FINANCIAL AND PERFORMANCE MANAGEMENT

More Reliable and Complete Information Needed to Address Federal Management and Fiscal Challenges

Why GAO Did This Study

To operate as effectively and efficiently as possible and to make difficult decisions to address the federal government's management and fiscal challenges, Congress, the administration, and federal managers must have ready access to reliable and complete financial and performance information—both for individual federal entities and programs and for government as a whole. GAO is required to annually audit the consolidated financial statements of the U.S. government. In addition, GAO is required to periodically report on federal agencies' efforts to increase the use of performance information in government and to take a more crosscutting and integrated perspective on performance.

This testimony presents the results of GAO's recent audits and reviews related to (1) the U.S. government's consolidated financial statements for fiscal year 2012, and (2) executive branch implementation of key provisions of the GPRA Modernization Act of 2010.

What GAO Recommends

Over the years, GAO has made numerous recommendations directed at improving federal financial management. The federal government has generally taken or plans to take actions to address GAO's recommendations. GAO has also made numerous recommendations to OMB to more fully implement the GPRA Modernization Act of 2010. OMB staff agreed with these recommendations.

View GAO-13-752T. For more information, contact Robert F. Dacey or Gary T. Engel at (202) 512-3406, or J. Christopher Mihm at (202) 512-6806.

What GAO Found

Three long-standing major impediments prevented GAO from expressing an opinion on the U.S. government's 2012 accrual-based consolidated financial statements: (1) serious financial management problems at the Department of Defense (DOD), (2) the federal government's inability to adequately account for and reconcile intragovernmental activity and balances between federal entities, and (3) the federal government's ineffective process for preparing the consolidated financial statements. Also, GAO was prevented from expressing opinions on the 2012 social insurance-related statements because of significant uncertainties primarily related to the achievement of projected reductions in Medicare cost growth reflected in the statements.

DOD continues to work to address its financial management challenges with the goal of full financial statement auditability, but has much work to do if the department is to meet its audit readiness and financial management improvement goals. In addition, the Department of the Treasury, in coordination with the Office of Management and Budget (OMB), is taking actions to address issues related to intragovernmental activity and preparation of the consolidated financial statements, but additional efforts and sustained commitment are required to fully resolve these issues.

The 2012 Financial Report of the United States Government included comprehensive long-term fiscal projections, which provide a much-needed perspective on the federal government's long-term fiscal position and outlook. These, like GAO's simulations, include the savings provided by the Budget Control Act of 2011, yet still show an unsustainable long-term fiscal path.

As GAO reported in June 2013, the executive branch has taken a number of steps to implement key provisions of the GPRA Modernization Act of 2010 (GPRAMA or the act), such as the development of interim cross-agency and agency-specific priority goals and use of data-driven quarterly performance reviews. However, the executive branch needs to do more to fully implement and leverage the act's provisions to address governance challenges in the following five areas: (1) OMB and agencies have made some progress addressing crosscutting issues, but are missing additional opportunities such as assessing the performance of tax expenditures; (2) while key performance management practices hold promise, ensuring performance information is useful and used by managers to improve results remains a weakness. For example, GAO found little improvement in federal managers' reported use of performance information or practices that could help promote its use, based on its periodic government-wide surveys of federal managers since 1997. Moreover, only 37 percent of managers reported that a program evaluation had been completed in the past 5 years of any program or operation they were involved in; (3) agencies have taken steps to align daily operations with agency results, but continue to face difficulties measuring performance in areas such as grants and contracts; (4) communication of performance information could better meet users' needs; and (5) agency performance information is not always useful for congressional decision making. GAO found little evidence that meaningful consultations occurred with Congress related to agency strategic plans and agency priority goals.

Chairman Issa, Ranking Member Cummings, and Members of the Committee:

I appreciate the opportunity to be here today to discuss our reports on the U.S. government's consolidated financial statements for fiscal years 2012 and 2011,[1] and on the federal government's progress in implementing the GPRA Modernization Act of 2010 (GPRAMA or the act).[2] The federal government is one of the world's largest and most complex entities, with about $3.5 trillion in outlays in fiscal year 2012, funding an extensive array of programs and operations. Moreover, it faces a number of significant fiscal, financial management, and performance management challenges in responding to the diverse and increasingly complex issues it seeks to address.

To operate as effectively and efficiently as possible and to make difficult decisions to address the federal government's management and fiscal challenges, Congress, the administration, and federal managers must have ready access to reliable and complete financial and performance information—both for individual federal entities and programs and for government as a whole. The government has made important progress since the enactment of key federal financial management reforms in the 1990s and continues to address significant financial management and long-term fiscal challenges. The act, which updated the Government Performance and Results Act of 1993 (GPRA),[3] was intended to help increase the use of performance information in government and to take a more crosscutting and integrated perspective on performance management. However, our reports on the U.S. government's consolidated financial statements and on the implementation of the act illustrate that further improvements to federal financial and performance management are urgently needed. I would like to commend you, Mr.

---

[1]The Secretary of the Treasury, in coordination with the Director of the Office of Management and Budget, is required to annually submit audited financial statements for the U.S. government to the President and Congress. GAO is required to audit these financial statements. The Government Management Reform Act of 1994 has required such reporting, covering the executive branch of government, beginning with the financial statements prepared for fiscal year 1997. 31 U.S.C. 331(e). The federal government has elected to include certain financial information on the legislative and judicial branches in the consolidated financial statements as well.

[2]Pub. L. No. 111-352, 124 Stat. 3866 (Jan. 4, 2011).

[3]Pub. L. No. 103-62, 107 Stat. 285 (Aug. 3, 1993).

Chairman, and this committee, for holding this oversight hearing on these important subjects. Congressional oversight is critical to assuring continued progress.

This testimony is based on several reports issued in 2013. In January 2013, we issued our report on the results of our audit of the U.S. government's fiscal years 2012 and 2011 consolidated financial statements, which along with the financial statements, are contained in the fiscal year *2012 Financial Report of the United States Government* (*Financial Report*).[4] We performed sufficient audit work to provide our report on the consolidated financial statements, internal control, and compliance with selected provisions of laws and regulations. We conducted our audit in accordance with U.S. generally accepted government auditing standards. Our audit report would not be possible without the commitment and professionalism of inspectors general throughout the federal government who are responsible for annually auditing the financial statements of individual federal entities.

The act includes provisions requiring us to review its implementation at several critical junctures.[5] In June 2013, we issued a report highlighting the key findings from several reports issued over the past 2 years covering the executive branch's implementation of key provisions of the act and how the executive branch can more fully implement and leverage the act to address pressing governance challenges.[6] The report also included the results of our most recent survey of federal managers on the implementation of key performance management practices across

---

[4]GAO, *Financial Audit: U.S. Government's Fiscal Years 2012 and 2011 Consolidated Financial Statements*, GAO-13-271R (Washington, D.C.: Jan. 17, 2013). The *Financial Report* is available through the Department of the Treasury at http://www.fms.treas.gov/fr/index.html. Also, see GAO, *Understanding the Primary Components of the Annual Financial Report of the United States Government*, GAO-09-946SP (Washington, D.C.: September 2009).

[5]For more information on our reports reviewing initial implementation of the act, see GAO, *Managing for Results: Executive Branch Should More Fully Implement the GPRA Modernization Act to Address Pressing Governance Challenges*, GAO-13-518 (Washington, D.C.: June 26, 2013). For more details on the scope and methodology for this work, see app. I of GAO-13-518.

[6]See GAO-13-518. For the full results of our 2013 survey, see GAO, *Managing for Results: 2013 Federal Managers Survey on Organization Performance and Management Issues, an E-Supplement to GAO-13-518*, GAO-13-519SP (Washington, D.C.: June 2013).

government—the fifth such survey we have undertaken since 1997. In addition to the survey, we reviewed the act, related Office of Management and Budget (OMB) guidance, and our past and recent work related to federal performance management and the act, as well as interviewed OMB staff. Based, in part, on some of the results of our federal managers' survey, we also issued a report in June 2013 on strategies to facilitate agencies' use of program evaluations.[7] In addition to the survey, we interviewed OMB staff and evaluators at five agencies within the Departments of Agriculture, Health and Human Services, and Labor selected for their evaluation experience. We conducted our performance audits in accordance with generally accepted government auditing standards.

Results of Our Audit of the U.S. Government's Consolidated Financial Statements for Fiscal Years 2012 and 2011

The federal government was unable to demonstrate the reliability of significant portions of its accrual-based consolidated financial statements for fiscal years 2012 and 2011, principally resulting from limitations related to certain material weaknesses in internal control over financial reporting.[8] For example, about 34 percent of the federal government's reported total assets as of September 30, 2012, and approximately 21 percent of the federal government's reported net cost for fiscal year 2012, relate to the Department of Defense (DOD), which received a disclaimer of opinion on its consolidated financial statements. As a result, we were unable to provide an opinion on the accrual-based consolidated financial statements of the U.S. government. Further, significant uncertainties, primarily related to the achievement of projected reductions in Medicare cost growth reflected in the 2012, 2011, and 2010 Statements of Social Insurance,[9] prevented us from expressing opinions on those

---

[7]GAO, *Program Evaluation: Strategies to Facilitate Agencies' Use of Evaluation in Program Management and Policy Making*, GAO-13-570 (Washington, D.C.: June 26, 2013). For more details on the scope and methodology for this work, see app. I of GAO-13-570.

[8]A material weakness is a deficiency, or combination of deficiencies, in internal control such that there is a reasonable possibility that a material misstatement of the entity's financial statements will not be prevented, or detected and corrected, on a timely basis. A deficiency in internal control exists when the design or operation of a control does not allow management or employees, in the normal course of performing their assigned functions, to prevent, or detect and correct, misstatements on a timely basis.

[9]These uncertainties are discussed in Note 26 to the consolidated financial statements.

statements,[10] as well as on the 2012 and 2011 Statements of Changes in Social Insurance Amounts. Given the importance of social insurance programs, such as Medicare and Social Security to the federal government's long-term fiscal outlook, the Statement of Social Insurance is critical to understanding the federal government's financial condition and fiscal sustainability.

The federal government did not maintain adequate systems or have sufficient, reliable evidence to support certain material information reported in the U.S. government's accrual-based consolidated financial statements. The underlying long-standing material weaknesses in internal control contributed to our disclaimers of opinion on the U.S. government's accrual-based consolidated financial statements for the fiscal years ended September 30, 2012 and 2011.[11] Specifically, these weaknesses concerned the federal government's inability to

- satisfactorily determine that property, plant, and equipment and inventories and related property, primarily held by DOD, were properly reported in the accrual-based consolidated financial statements;

- reasonably estimate or adequately support the amounts reported for certain liabilities, such as environmental and disposal liabilities, or determine whether commitments and contingencies were complete and properly reported;

- support significant portions of the reported total net cost of operations, most notably related to DOD, and adequately reconcile disbursement activity at certain federal entities;

- adequately account for and reconcile intragovernmental activity and balances between federal entities;

- ensure that the federal government's accrual-based consolidated financial statements were (1) consistent with the underlying audited

---

[10]We expressed unqualified opinions on the 2009 and 2008 Statements of Social Insurance.

[11]A more detailed description of the material weaknesses that contributed to our disclaimer of opinion, including the primary effects of these material weaknesses on the accrual-based consolidated financial statements and on the management of federal government operations, can be found on pages 237 through 242 of the *Financial Report*.

entities' financial statements, (2) properly balanced, and (3) in conformity with U.S. generally accepted accounting principles (U.S. GAAP); and

- identify and either resolve or explain material differences between (1) components of the budget deficit that are used to prepare certain information in the consolidated financial statements and (2) related amounts reported in federal entities' financial statements and underlying financial information and records.

These material weaknesses continued to (1) hamper the federal government's ability to reliably report a significant portion of its assets, liabilities, costs, and other related information; (2) affect the federal government's ability to reliably measure the full cost as well as the financial and nonfinancial performance of certain programs and activities; (3) impair the federal government's ability to adequately safeguard significant assets and properly record various transactions; and (4) hinder the federal government from having reliable financial information to operate in an efficient and effective manner.

We also reported certain other material weaknesses,[12] including the federal government's inability to (1) determine the full extent to which improper payments occur and reasonably assure that appropriate actions are taken to reduce improper payments,[13] and (2) identify and resolve information security control deficiencies and manage information security risks on an ongoing basis.

Since the enactment of key financial management reforms in the 1990s, important progress has been made improving financial management activities and practices. For fiscal year 2012, 21 of 24 Chief Financial Officers (CFO) Act agencies were able to attain unqualified audit opinions on their accrual-based financial statements, up from 6 CFO Act agencies for fiscal year 1996.[14] Also, for the first time, the Department of Homeland

---

[12]A more detailed discussion of these weaknesses, including the primary effects of the material weaknesses on the accrual-based consolidated financial statements and on the management of federal government operations, can be found on pages 243 through 245 of the *Financial Report*.

[13]Federal entities reported estimates of improper payment amounts that totaled $107.7 billion for fiscal year 2012, which represented approximately 4.4 percent of about $2.5 trillion of reported outlays for the associated programs.

[14]See app. I for the fiscal year 2012 audit results for the 24 CFO Act Agencies.

GAO-13-752T

Security (DHS) was able to obtain a qualified audit opinion on its department-wide financial statements—a significant achievement for DHS. Further, the preparation and audit of financial statements have identified numerous deficiencies, leading to actions to strengthen controls and systems. However, many of the CFO Act agencies continue to struggle with financial systems that do not meet the needs of management for reliable, useful, and timely financial information.

The Federal Financial Management Improvement Act of 1996 (FFMIA) was designed to lead to system improvements that would result in CFO Act agency managers routinely having access to reliable, useful, and timely financial-related information with which to measure performance and increase accountability throughout the year.[15] FFMIA requires auditors, as part of the 24 CFO Act agencies' financial statement audits, to report whether those agencies' financial management systems substantially comply with (1) federal financial management systems requirements, (2) applicable federal accounting standards, and (3) the federal government's *U.S. Standard General Ledger* at the transaction level.

For both fiscal years 2012 and 2011, auditors for 11 of the 24 CFO Act agencies reported that the agencies' financial management systems did not substantially comply with one or more of the three FFMIA requirements. Often, federal entities expend major time, effort, and resources to develop financial information that their systems should be able to provide on a daily or recurring basis. Therefore, it is important for the individual federal entities to remain committed to maintaining the progress that has been achieved in obtaining positive audit results and to build upon that progress to make needed improvements in federal financial management systems.

Addressing Impediments to an Opinion on the Accrual-Based Consolidated Financial Statements

Three long-standing major impediments continued to prevent us from expressing an opinion on the U.S. government's accrual-based consolidated financial statements: (1) serious financial management problems at DOD, (2) the federal government's inability to adequately account for and reconcile intragovernmental activity and balances

---

[15]FFMIA, which is reprinted in 31 U.S.C. 3512 note.

between federal entities, and (3) the federal government's ineffective process for preparing the consolidated financial statements.

Improving Financial Management at DOD

DOD continues to work toward the long-term goal of improving financial management and full financial statement auditability. The National Defense Authorization Act (NDAA) for Fiscal Year 2010 requires that DOD's Financial Improvement and Audit Readiness (FIAR) Plan set as its goal that the department's financial statements be validated as ready for audit by September 30, 2017.[16] In addition, the NDAA for Fiscal Year 2013 requires that the FIAR Plan also describe specific actions to be taken and the cost associated with ensuring that DOD's Statement of Budgetary Resources (SBR) is validated as ready for audit by September 30, 2014.[17] DOD's FIAR Plan and semiannual status reports define the activities, corrective actions, and interim milestones the department has deemed necessary to achieve auditability and the availability of reliable, useful, and timely information for management decision making. Under its FIAR Plan, DOD is focusing on improving controls, systems, and processes relied on to provide financial information in two areas that are critical to managing its operations: (1) budgetary information and (2) accountability over its mission-critical assets.

Based on difficulties encountered in auditing the SBR of the Marine Corps, in August 2012, DOD's FIAR Governance Board approved a significant change to the FIAR methodology that will limit the scope of first-year SBR audits for all DOD components. As outlined in the March 2013 revised FIAR Guidance, the scope of the SBR audits beginning in fiscal year 2015 will be on budget activity only in the current-year appropriations as an interim step toward achieving an audit of the SBR. In subsequent years, the components will commence audits of schedules of both current-year and prior-year audited appropriations and all related activity against those appropriated funds.

---

[16]Pub. L. No. 111-84, § 1003(a)(2)(A)(ii), 123 Stat. 2190, 2440 (Oct. 28, 2009) (reprinted in 10 U.S.C. § 2222 note). Prior to enactment of this law, DOD had been using the September 30, 2017 date as its internal goal since 2008.

[17]NDAA for Fiscal Year 2013, Pub. L. No. 112-239, § 1005(a), 126 Stat. 1632, 1904 (Jan. 2, 2013) (reprinted in 10 U.S.C. § 2222 note).

While DOD has made efforts to improve its financial management, we found significant internal control, financial management, and systems deficiencies in DOD's processes and procedures for maintaining accountability for billions of dollars in funds and other resources. For example, we found that

- the Army and the Defense Finance and Accounting Service (DFAS) could not readily identify the full population of payroll accounts associated with the Army's $46 billion active duty military payroll because of deficiencies in existing procedures and nonintegrated personnel and payroll systems,[18]

- DFAS could not detect and correct all errors in active duty military payroll disbursements because of deficiencies in its processes,[19]

- DOD's improper payment estimates reported in its fiscal year 2011 *Agency Financial Report* were neither reliable nor statistically valid because of long-standing and pervasive financial management weaknesses and significant deficiencies in the department's procedures related to estimating improper payments,[20] and

- DOD continues to encounter difficulties in implementing its planned Enterprise Resource Planning (ERP) systems on schedule and within budget,[21] due to significant operational problems and significant delays in deploying key ERP systems.[22]

---

[18]GAO, *DOD Financial Management: The Army Faces Significant Challenges in Achieving Audit Readiness for Its Military Pay*, GAO-12-406 (Washington, D.C.: Mar. 22, 2012).

[19]GAO, *DOD Financial Management: Actions Needed to Address Deficiencies in Controls over Army Active Duty Military Payroll*, GAO-13-28 (Washington, D.C.: Dec. 12, 2012).

[20]GAO, *DOD Financial Management: Significant Improvements Needed in Efforts to Address Improper Payment Requirements*, GAO-13-227 (Washington, D.C.: May 13, 2013).

[21]The effective implementation of ERP systems will be critical to the success of all of DOD's planned long-term financial improvement efforts. ERP systems are integrated, multifunction systems that perform business-related tasks such as general ledger accounting and supply chain management. DOD considers their implementation essential to transforming its business operations and achieving its goals of audit readiness by fiscal year 2017.

[22]GAO, *DOD Financial Management: Implementation Weaknesses in Army and Air Force Business Systems Could Jeopardize DOD's Auditability Goals*, GAO-12-134 (Washington, D.C.: Feb. 28, 2012).

We have made numerous recommendations to DOD to address these financial management issues. While we are encouraged by DOD's sustained commitment to improving financial management and achieving audit readiness, several DOD business practices, including financial management, remain on GAO's list of high-risk programs.[23] DOD faces considerable challenges and has much work to do if it is to meet its audit readiness goals. DOD's continued oversight and monitoring will play a key role in ensuring that the FIAR Plan is implemented as intended, and lessons learned are identified and effectively disseminated and addressed.[24] While DOD's May 2013 FIAR Plan status report reiterated the department's commitment to achieving its audit readiness goals, it noted that absent a stable budget environment, DOD's efforts were subject to increased risk. Continued congressional oversight of DOD's financial management improvement efforts will be critical to helping ensure DOD achieves its audit readiness goals. To assist Congress in its oversight efforts, we will continue to monitor DOD's progress and provide feedback on the status of its financial management improvement efforts.

Reconciling Intragovernmental Activity and Balances

Since the first audit of the U.S. government's fiscal year 1997 consolidated financial statements, we have reported a material weakness related to the federal government's inability to adequately account for and reconcile intragovernmental activity and balances between federal entities, as well as between federal entities and the General Fund.[25] When preparing the consolidated financial statements, intragovernmental activity and balances between federal entities and between federal entities and the General Fund should be in agreement and must be subtracted out, or eliminated, from the financial statements. If the two federal entities engaged in an intragovernmental transaction do not both record the same intragovernmental transaction in the same year and for the same amount, the intragovernmental transactions will not be in agreement, resulting in errors in the consolidated financial statements.

---

[23]GAO, *High-Risk Series: An Update*, GAO-13-283 (Washington, D.C.: Feb. 14, 2013).

[24]GAO, *DOD Financial Management: Challenges in Attaining Audit Readiness and Improving Business Processes and Systems*, GAO-12-642T (Washington, D.C.: Apr. 18, 2012).

[25]The General Fund is a central reporting entity that tracks core activities fundamental to funding the federal government (e.g., issued budget authority, operating cash, and debt financing activities).

The Department of the Treasury (Treasury) has grouped intragovernmental activity and balances into the following five categories and is working with federal entity personnel to identify and resolve reported unreconciled differences.

- **Fiduciary activities** include investments in Treasury securities with the Bureau of the Fiscal Service (Fiscal Service),[26] borrowing from the Fiscal Service and the Federal Financing Bank and related interest receivable and payable, interest expense and revenue, and federal loans receivable and payable.

- **Benefit activities** include contributions by federal entities into employee benefit programs (retirement, life insurance, workers' compensation, and health benefits) administered by the Office of Personnel Management and the Department of Labor.

- **Buy/Sell activities** between federal entities include buy and sell costs and revenues, accounts receivable and payable, and advances to and from others.

- **Transfers of funds** include transfers payable and receivable, and transfers in and out without reimbursement.

- **General Fund transactions and balances** include fund balance with Treasury, appropriations received and warrants, and custodial and non-entity collections.

The federal government has made progress in reconciling intragovernmental differences and the degree of progress varies by category. However, the federal government continues to be unable to adequately account for and reconcile intragovernmental activity and balances. For fiscal year 2012, amounts reported by federal entity trading partners for certain intragovernmental accounts were not in agreement by significant amounts. OMB and Treasury require the CFOs of 35 significant federal entities to reconcile, on a quarterly basis, selected

---

[26]According to Treasury officials, on October 7, 2012, the Secretary of the Treasury (1) established the Bureau of the Fiscal Service as a bureau within the Department of the Treasury, (2) consolidated and redesignated the Bureau of the Public Debt and the Financial Management Service as the Bureau of the Fiscal Service, and (3) transferred the duties of the Bureau of the Public Debt and Financial Management Service commissioners to the Commissioner of the Bureau of the Fiscal Service.

intragovernmental activity and balances with their trading partners. As in prior years, a substantial number of the entities did not adequately perform the required year-end reconciliations for fiscal year 2012. Further, there continue to be hundreds of billions of dollars of unreconciled differences between the General Fund of the U.S. government and federal entity trading partners related to appropriations and other intragovernmental transactions. Currently, federal entities report their activity with the General Fund; however, the General Fund activity is not centrally reported, and therefore, a process does not exist for entities to confirm and reconcile all of their activity and balances with the General Fund. As a result of these circumstances, the federal government's ability to determine the impact of the unreconciled differences between trading partners on the amounts reported in the accrual-based consolidated financial statements is significantly impaired.

Over the years, we have made several recommendations to Treasury to address these issues. Treasury has taken or plans to take actions to address these recommendations. During fiscal year 2012, Treasury expanded its ongoing efforts to help resolve and eliminate material differences in intragovernmental activity and balances. These efforts included developing and implementing a formalized resolution plan and related corrective actions intended to address long-standing intragovernmental challenges. As part of its plan, Treasury monitors entities' reconciliation efforts and compliance with *Treasury Financial Manual* guidance. For example, in fiscal year 2012, Treasury began a pilot program with 14 entities that included providing them with quarterly metrics and scorecards highlighting differences requiring attention. In fiscal year 2013, Treasury expanded the distribution of the quarterly metrics and scorecards to include all 35 significant entities. Further, Treasury is in the process of establishing separate reporting for the General Fund, which includes intragovernmental transactions. Resolving the intragovernmental transactions problem remains a difficult challenge and will require a strong and sustained commitment by federal entities to timely resolve differences with their trading partners, as well as continued strong leadership by Treasury and OMB.

Preparing the Consolidated Financial Statements

Treasury, in coordination with OMB, implemented corrective actions during fiscal year 2012 to address certain internal control deficiencies detailed in our previously issued reports regarding the process for preparing the consolidated financial statements, including obtaining and utilizing certain interim financial information from federal entities in preparing initial consolidated financial statement drafts and supplementing staff during the financial report preparation process.

Treasury also began to develop a methodology to reconcile the budget deficit to the consolidated financial statements. Nevertheless, the federal government continued to have inadequate systems, controls, and procedures to ensure that the consolidated financial statements are consistent with the underlying audited entity financial statements, properly balanced, and in conformity with U.S. GAAP.[27] For example:

- Treasury's process did not ensure that the information in three of the accrual-based consolidated financial statements (Statement of Operations and Changes in Net Position, Reconciliations of Net Operating Cost and Unified Budget Deficit, and Statement of Changes in Cash Balance from Unified Budget and Other Activities) was fully consistent with the underlying information in the 35 significant federal entities' audited financial statements and other financial data.

- Treasury is unable to properly balance the accrual-based consolidated financial statements. To make the fiscal years 2012 and 2011 consolidated financial statements balance, Treasury recorded net increases of $20.2 billion and $15.6 billion, respectively, to net operating cost on the Statement of Operations and Changes in Net Position, which were identified as "Unmatched transactions and balances."[28] Treasury recorded an additional net $1.8 billion and $6.0 billion of unmatched transactions in the Statement of Net Cost for fiscal years 2012 and 2011, respectively. The material weakness in federal entities' ability to account for and reconcile intragovernmental activity and balances, discussed above, significantly contributes to the unmatched transactions and balances and consequently impairs Treasury's ability to fully eliminate such intragovernmental activity and balances.

---

[27]Most of the issues we identified in fiscal year 2012 existed in fiscal year 2011, and many have existed for a number of years. Most recently, in June 2013, we reported the issues we identified to Treasury and OMB and provided recommendations for corrective action. See GAO, *Management Report: Improvements Needed in Controls over the Preparation of the U.S. Consolidated Financial Statements*, GAO-13-540 (Washington, D.C.: June 28, 2013). A detailed discussion of control deficiencies regarding the process for preparing the consolidated financial statements can be found on pages 239 through 241 of the *Financial Report*.

[28]Although Treasury was unable to determine how much of the unmatched transactions and balances, if any, relates to net operating cost, it reported this amount as a component of net operating cost in the consolidated financial statements.

- Treasury's reporting of certain financial information required by U.S. GAAP continues to be impaired and will remain so until federal entities, such as DOD, can provide Treasury with complete and reliable information required to be reported in the consolidated financial statements.

Resolving these internal control deficiencies remains a difficult challenge and will require a strong and sustained commitment from Treasury and OMB as they continue to execute and implement their corrective action plans.

Significant Uncertainties Result in Disclaimers of Opinion on the 2012, 2011, and 2010 Statements of Social Insurance, as Well as on the 2012 and 2011 Statements of Changes in Social Insurance Amounts

Significant uncertainties, primarily related to the achievement of projected reductions in Medicare cost growth reflected in the 2012, 2011, and 2010 Statements of Social Insurance, prevented us from expressing opinions on the 2012, 2011, and 2010 Statements of Social Insurance, as well as on the 2012 and 2011 Statements of Changes in Social Insurance Amounts.[29] The Statement of Social Insurance presents the actuarial present value of the federal government's estimated future revenue to be received from or on behalf of participants and estimated future expenditures to be paid to or on behalf of participants, based on benefit formulas in current law and using a projection period sufficient to illustrate the long-term sustainability of the social insurance programs.[30]

These significant uncertainties include the following:

- Medicare projections in the 2012, 2011, and 2010 Statements of Social Insurance were based on benefit formulas in current law and included a significant decrease in projected Medicare costs from the 2009 Statement of Social Insurance related to (1) reductions in Medicare payment rates for physician services (totaling almost 31 percent in January 2013, as estimated in the *2012 Medicare Trustees*

---

[29]About $27.2 trillion, or 70.5 percent, of the federal government's reported total present value of future expenditures in excess of future revenue presented in the 2012 Statement of Social Insurance relates to Medicare programs reported in the Department of Health and Human Services' 2012 Statement of Social Insurance, which received a disclaimer of opinion.

[30]The projection period used for the Social Security, Medicare, and Railroad Retirement social insurance programs is 75 years. For the Black Lung program, the projections are through September 30, 2040.

Report)[31] and (2) productivity improvements for most other categories of Medicare providers, based on full implementation of the provisions of the Patient Protection and Affordable Care Act, as amended (PPACA).[32] However, there are significant uncertainties concerning the achievement of these projected decreases in Medicare costs.

- As discussed in note 26 in the *Financial Report*, actual future costs for Medicare are likely to exceed those shown by the current-law projections presented in the 2012, 2011, and 2010 Statements of Social Insurance due, for example, to the likelihood of modifications to the scheduled reductions in Medicare payment rates for physician services.[33] The extent to which actual future costs exceed the projected current-law amounts due to changes to the scheduled reductions in Medicare payment rates for physician services and productivity adjustments depends on both the specific changes that might be legislated and whether such legislation would include further provisions to help offset such costs.

- The *Financial Report* includes an illustrative alternative projection that is intended to provide additional context regarding the long-term sustainability of the Medicare program and to illustrate the uncertainties in the Statement of Social Insurance projections. The present value of future estimated expenditures in excess of future estimated revenue for Medicare, included in the illustrative alternative projection, exceeds the $27.2 trillion estimate in the 2012 Statement of Social Insurance by $10.1 trillion.

Projections of Medicare costs are sensitive to assumptions about future decisions by policymakers and about the behavioral responses of consumers, employers, and health care providers as policy, incentives,

---

[31]Subsequent to our audit, the *2013 Medicare Trustees Report* was issued on May 31, 2013.

[32]PPACA, Pub. L. No. 111-148, 124 Stat. 119 (Mar. 23, 2010), as amended by the Health Care and Education Reconciliation Act of 2010, Pub. L. No. 111-152, 124 Stat. 1029 (Mar. 30, 2010).

[33]Statutes have been enacted with provisions that prevented scheduled reductions in Medicare payment rates for physician services from taking effect from 2003 through 2013, including the most recent provision enacted in the American Taxpayer Relief Act of 2012 (ATRA), Pub. L. No. 112-240, § 601, 126 Stat. 2313, 2345 (Jan. 2, 2013). Some of these statutes also included provisions that reduced the federal government's spending on other categories of health care, which had the effect of helping to offset the increased costs related to the physician payment updates.

and the health care sector change over time. Such secondary impacts are not fully reflected in the Statement of Social Insurance projections but could be expected to influence the excess cost growth rate used in the projections.[34] Key drivers of uncertainty about the excess cost growth rate include the future development and deployment of medical technology, the evolution of personal income, and the cost and availability of insurance, as well as federal policy changes, such as the implementation of PPACA. Both the Statement of Social Insurance projections and the illustrative alternative estimate summarized in Note 26 in the *Financial Report* indicate that the Social Security and Medicare programs are not sustainable under current financing arrangements.

Long-Term Fiscal Challenges

The 2012 *Financial Report* includes comprehensive fiscal projections for the U.S. government that, consistent with GAO simulations, show that without changes in current policy, the federal government continues to face an unsustainable long-term fiscal path.[35] Such reporting provides a much needed perspective on the federal government's long-term fiscal position and outlook. The projections included in the *Financial Report* and our simulations both continue to highlight the need to focus attention not only on the federal government's near-term budget outlook but also on its longer-term fiscal path. In the near term, deficits are expected to continue to decline from the recent historic highs as the economy recovers and actions taken by Congress and the President begin to take effect. Debt held by the public as a share of gross domestic product (GDP), however, remains well above historical averages. Debt held by the public at these high levels could limit the federal government's flexibility to address emerging issues and unforeseen challenges such as another economic downturn or large-scale natural disaster.

---

[34]The excess cost growth rate is the increase in health care spending per person relative to the growth of gross domestic product per person after removing the effects of demographic changes on health care spending.

[35]GAO, *The Federal Government's Long-Term Fiscal Outlook, Spring 2013 Update*, GAO-13-481SP (Washington, D.C.: Apr. 11, 2013), and *The Federal Government's Long-Term Fiscal Outlook: Fall 2012 Update*, GAO-13-148SP (Washington, D.C.: Dec. 3, 2012). The key difference between these two is that the Spring 2013 update reflects the enactment of ATRA, which among other changes, modified the 2013 and 2014 discretionary spending limits, permanently extended many of the tax provisions that were previously set to expire under current law and limited the reach of the Alternative Minimum Tax. The overall effects of ATRA on the longer-term outlook under GAO's alternative simulation are relatively small.

Both the projections in the *Financial Report* and our long-term simulations reflect enactment of the Budget Control Act of 2011 (BCA).[36] BCA set limits on discretionary spending for fiscal years 2012 through 2021. Under the enacted discretionary spending limits, discretionary spending as a share of the economy in 2021 would be lower than any level seen in the last 50 years. Even with the reductions from BCA, the government continues to face a significant structural imbalance between revenues and spending, driven on the spending side largely by the aging of the population and rising health care costs. Changing this path will not be easy, and it will likely require difficult decisions affecting both federal spending and revenue. Significant action to change the long-term path must be taken soon to minimize the risk that eventual policy changes will be disruptive to individuals and the economy, while also taking into account concerns about near-term economic growth.

The Executive Branch Needs to More Fully Implement the GPRA Modernization Act to Address Pressing Governance Challenges

As we reported in June 2013, the executive branch has taken a number of steps to implement key provisions of the GPRA Modernization Act of 2010 (the act). OMB has developed interim cross-agency priority goals, and agencies developed agency-specific priority goals.[37] Agency officials reported that their agencies have assigned performance management leadership roles and responsibilities to officials, such as performance improvement officers, who generally participate in performance management activities, including data-driven quarterly performance reviews. Further, OMB developed Performance.gov, a government-wide website, which provides quarterly updates on the cross-agency priority goals and agency priority goals. The Performance Improvement Council, which consists of agency performance improvement officers, has also taken steps to facilitate the exchange of useful practices and tips and tools to strengthen agency performance management. Nevertheless, our work has shown that the executive branch needs to do more to fully implement and leverage the act's provisions to address governance challenges.

---

[36]The Budget Control Act of 2011, Pub. L. No. 112-25, § 302, 125 Stat. 240, 256-59 (Aug. 2, 2011), *classified, as amended, in* 2 U.S.C. § 901a.

[37]GAO-13-518.

OMB and Agencies Have Made Some Progress Addressing Crosscutting Issues but Are Missing Additional Opportunities

Many of the meaningful results that the federal government seeks to achieve, such as those related to protecting food and agriculture and providing homeland security, require the coordinated efforts of more than one federal agency, level of government, or sector. For almost two decades we have reported on agencies' missed opportunities for improved collaboration through the effective implementation of GPRA. Under the act, OMB and agencies have identified many programs and activities that contribute to goals, as required, but our recent work continues to show that they are missing additional opportunities to address crosscutting issues. While agencies have implemented some of the act's provisions, their efforts have not included all of the relevant agency, program, and other contributors. For example, few have identified tax expenditures, which represent about $1 trillion in foregone revenue in fiscal year 2012, due to a lack of OMB guidance and oversight. Therefore, the contributions made by tax expenditures toward broader federal outcomes are unknown. In June 2013, we recommended that OMB take several actions to ensure that the contributions of tax expenditures to crosscutting and agency goals are identified and assessed.[38] OMB staff agreed with these recommendations.

In addition, agencies are not consistently including all relevant stakeholders as they implement key provisions of the act in the following areas:

- **Cross-agency priority goals:** In May 2012, we identified additional agencies that should be named as contributors for 10 of the 14 interim cross-agency priority goals.[39]

- **Agency priority goals:** In April 2013, we found that agencies identified contributors within the agency for each agency priority goal, but did not identify external contributors for 29 of the 102 agency priority goals we reviewed. In some cases, the goals seem to be internally focused, but in other cases, our work has shown that there are external contributors that were not listed.[40]

---

[38]GAO-13-518.

[39]GAO, *Managing for Results: GAO's Work Related to the Interim Crosscutting Priority Goals under the GPRA Modernization Act*, GAO-12-620R (Washington, D.C.: May 31, 2012).

[40]GAO, *Managing for Results: Agencies Should More Fully Develop Priority Goals under the GPRA Modernization Act*, GAO-13-174 (Washington, D.C.: Apr. 19, 2013).

- **Quarterly performance reviews:** In February 2013, we reported that while we found that quarterly performance reviews have shown promise in improving internal agency coordination and collaboration, few agency performance improvement officers reported that they were using the reviews to coordinate or collaborate with other agencies that have similar goals.[41]

We made recommendations to the Director of OMB to address each of these areas. OMB staff agreed with these recommendations.

Ensuring Performance Information Is Useful and Used by Managers to Improve Results Remains a Weakness, but Key Performance Management Practices Hold Promise

As we reported in June 2013, we found little improvement in federal managers' reported use of performance information or practices that could help promote its use, based on our periodic government-wide surveys of federal managers since 1997. In particular, as figure 1 illustrates, the results from our 2013 managers survey show almost no statistically significant changes in managers' perceptions of their leaders' and supervisors' attention and commitment to use of performance information since our last survey in 2007—with the exception of a decline in the percentage of managers who agreed to a great or very great extent that their agencies' top leadership demonstrates a strong commitment to achieving results.

---

[41]GAO, *Managing for Results: Data-Driven Performance Reviews Show Promise But Agencies Should Explore How to Involve Other Relevant Agencies*, GAO-13-228 (Washington, D.C.: Feb. 27, 2013).

Figure 1: Less Than Two-Thirds of Federal Managers Agreed in 2013 to a "Great" or "Very Great" Extent with Statements about Leadership and Supervisor Commitment and Attention to Performance Information

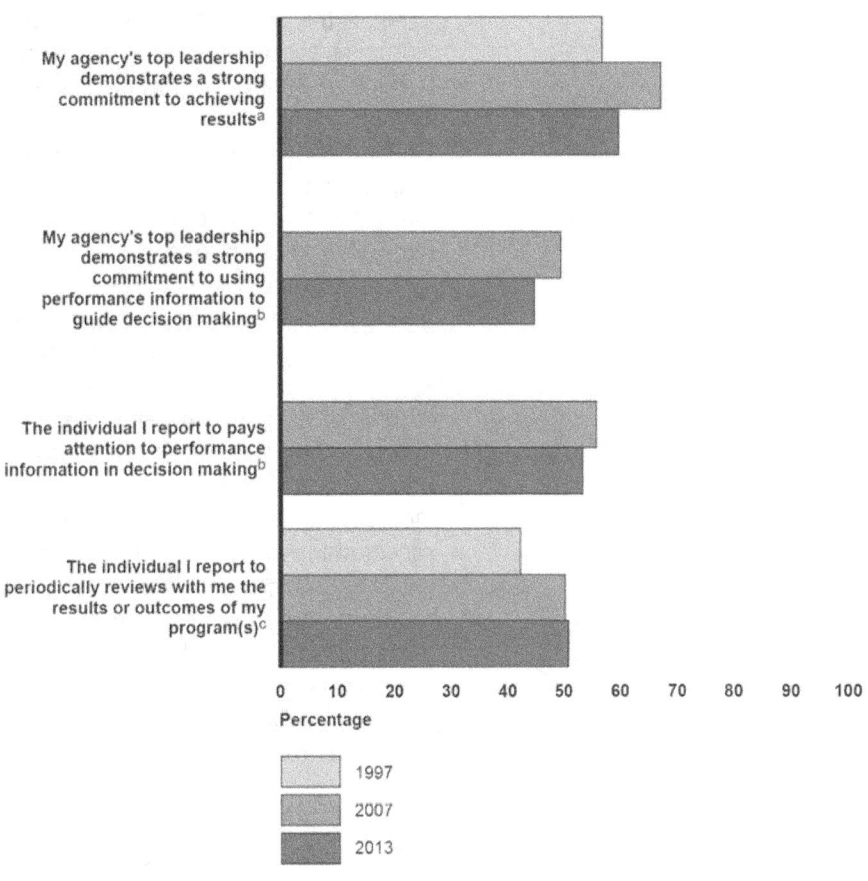

Source: GAO.

Notes: Percentage estimates for 2013 and 2007 have 95 percent confidence intervals within +/- 4 percentage points of the estimate, and percentage estimates for 1997 have confidence intervals within +/- 6.1 percentage points of the estimate.

Some survey items were abbreviated. For the full text, see items 10g, 10h, 11a, and 12c in GAO-13-519SP.

[a]Statistically significant decrease between 2007 and 2013.

[b]Survey item was introduced in 2007.

[c]Statistically significant increase between 1997 and 2013.

Importantly, agencies' quarterly performance reviews show promise as a leadership strategy for improving the use of performance information in agencies. According to our 2012 survey of performance improvement officers at 24 agencies, the majority (21 out of 24 agencies required to conduct these reviews) reported that actionable opportunities for performance improvement are identified through the reviews at least half the time.[42] In addition, most officials we interviewed at the Department of Energy, the Department of the Treasury, and the Small Business Administration attributed improvements in performance and decision making to their performance reviews.

Building the capacity to use performance information is also critical to helping ensure that information is used in a meaningful fashion, and inadequate staff expertise, among other factors, can hinder agencies' use. Only about a third (36 percent) of federal managers reported in our 2013 survey that they agreed to a great or very great extent that their agencies have sufficient analytical tools for managers at their levels to collect, analyze, and use performance information. The act lays out specific requirements for the Office of Personnel Management (OPM) to identify skills and competencies for performance management functions, among other actions. OPM has identified competencies and relevant position classifications and taken steps to work with agencies to incorporate the key competencies into agency training. However, we reported in April 2013 that these efforts have been broad-based and not informed by specific assessments of agency training needs.[43] We recommended that the Director of OPM work with the Performance Improvement Council to identify competency gaps for agency performance management staff and use this information to identify and share relevant agency training. OPM agreed with these recommendations.

Our 2013 government-wide survey found that most managers also lack recent program evaluation studies—a particular form of performance information—that can identify ways to improve program efficiency and effectiveness.[44] Only 37 percent of managers reported that an evaluation had been completed in the past 5 years of any program or operation they

---

[42]GAO-13-356 and GAO-13-228.

[43]GAO-13-356.

[44]GAO, *Program Evaluation: Strategies to Facilitate Agencies' Use of Evaluation in Program Management and Policy Making*, GAO-13-570 (Washington, D.C.: June 26, 2013). Program evaluations are systematic studies that use research methods to assess the achievement of a program's objectives in context, to explore the reasons for observed results and isolate program effects from other influences.

were involved in. Yet, 81 percent of the managers who had evaluations reported that evaluations contributed to a moderate or greater extent to implementing changes to improve program management or performance.

As you know, we have issued three reports outlining numerous areas of potential fragmentation, overlap and duplication in federal programs.[45] Comprehensive program evaluations that examine the coverage and effectiveness of a cluster of federal programs and policies aimed at achieving similar outcomes could be key in coordinating and streamlining programs so as to reduce duplication and overlap. In case study interviews, agency evaluators emphasized three basic strategies to facilitate evaluation influence on program management and policy making: (1) demonstrate leadership support by promoting the use of evidence and funding evaluation offices to promote and support the use of evidence; (2) build a strong body of evidence by attending to rigor in whatever methods are used; and (3) engage stakeholders throughout the evaluation process—gaining their input to planning; providing assistance, training, and incentives; and disseminating usable messages.

Agencies Have Taken Steps to Align Daily Operations with Agency Results but Continue to Face Difficulties Measuring Performance

Agencies have established performance management systems to align individual performance with agency results. However, agencies continue to face long-standing issues with measuring performance, such as obtaining complete, timely, and accurate performance information, across various programs and activities. Given the Performance Improvement Council's responsibilities for addressing crosscutting performance issues and sharing performance improvement practices, our June 2013 report noted that it could do more to examine and address the difficulties agencies face to measuring performance across various program types,

---

[45]GAO, *2013 Annual Report: Actions Needed to Reduce Fragmentation, Overlap, and Duplication and Achieve Other Financial Benefits*, GAO-13-279SP (Washington, D.C.: Apr. 9, 2013); *2012 Annual Report: Opportunities to Reduce Duplication, Overlap and Fragmentation, Achieve Savings, and Enhance Revenue*, GAO-12-342SP (Washington D.C.: Feb. 28, 2012); and *Opportunities to Reduce Potential Duplication in Government Programs, Save Tax Dollars, and Enhance Revenue*, GAO-11-318SP (Washington, D.C.: Mar. 1, 2011).

such as grants and contracts.[46,47] We recommended that OMB work with the Performance Improvement Council to develop a detailed approach for addressing these long-standing performance measurement issues. OMB staff agreed with this recommendation.

Communication of Performance Information Could Better Meet Users' Needs

Federal managers and potential users of Performance.gov reported concerns about the accessibility, availability, understandability, and relevance of performance information to the public. Potential users include Members and committees of Congress and the public. In our June 2013 report reviewing Performance.gov, we noted that the website has the potential to increase the accessibility of performance information for users both inside and outside the federal government.[48] However, further outreach to key stakeholders could help improve how this information is communicated. We recommended in June 2013 that OMB work with the Performance Improvement Council and the General Services Administration, which are involved in the development of the website, to (1) clarify the specific ways that intended audiences could use the information on Performance.gov and (2) systematically collect information on the needs of intended audiences and collect recommended performance metrics that help identify improvements to the website. OMB staff agreed with these recommendations.

Agency Performance Information Is Not Always Useful for Congressional Decision Making

Our work has found that the performance information that agencies provided to the Congress was not always useful for congressional decision making because the information was not clear, directly relevant, or sufficiently detailed. Consultations with Congress are intended, in part, to ensure that performance information is useful for congressional decision making. OMB and agencies are to consult with relevant committees, including this committee, about proposed goals at least once every 2 years. Specifically, OMB is to consult about the cross-agency

---

[46]GAO-13-518.

[47]We also recommended in April 2013 that the Director of OMB work with the Performance Improvement Council to gather regular feedback from its members on its performance and update its strategic plan, as appropriate. OMB staff agreed with these recommendations; see GAO-13-356.

[48]GAO, *Managing for Results: Leading Practices Should Guide the Continued Development of Performance.gov*, GAO-13-517 (Washington, D.C.: June 6, 2013).

priority goals and describe on Performance.gov how congressional input was incorporated into these goals. Similarly, agencies are to consult about their strategic plans, including agency priority goals, and describe in these plans or on Performance.gov, respectively, how that input was incorporated. However, in April 2013 we found little evidence that meaningful consultations occurred related to agency strategic plans and agency priority goals.[49] We recommended that the Director of OMB ensure that agencies provide a description of how input from congressional consultations was incorporated into each priority goal. OMB staff concurred with our recommendation.

In February 2014, OMB and agencies will publish a new set of cross-agency priority goals, agency priority goals, and updated agency strategic plans. According to OMB guidance, agency consultations with Congress, including this committee, on updated strategic plans and agency priority goals should take place this summer. Similarly, OMB has stated plans to consult with this committee and other committees with broad jurisdiction on the next set of cross-agency priority goals prior to their publication. At the request of Congress, we developed a guide in June 2012 to assist Members of Congress and their staffs in ensuring that the consultations required under the act are useful for assessing agency performance.[50] The guide outlines general approaches for successful consultations and key questions that Members of Congress and congressional staffs can ask as part of the consultation process.

Closing Comments

In closing, while progress has been made, much work remains given the federal government's long-term fiscal, financial management, and performance management challenges. Congress, the administration, and federal managers need to have more reliable, useful, and timely financial and performance information to effectively meet these challenges, to make sound decisions, and to operate as efficiently and effectively as possible. Agencies must continue to strive toward routinely producing such information to help guide decision makers on a day-to-day basis. Federal entities' improvement of financial management systems will be

---

[49]GAO-13-174.

[50]GAO, *Managing for Results: A Guide for Using the GPRA Modernization Act to Help Inform Congressional Decision Making*, GAO-12-621SP (Washington, D.C.: June 15, 2012).

essential to achieve this goal for their agency and the government as a whole.

Meaningful improvement in financial and performance management will not occur without sustained commitment by executive branch leaders and managers and continued oversight by Congress. The single most important element of successful financial and performance management improvement efforts is the demonstrated commitment of top leaders. This commitment is most prominently shown through the personal involvement of leaders, especially with agency data-driven performance reviews. Demonstrating leadership support for accountability and improvement by promoting capacity building and the use of evidence is also essential in helping facilitate program evaluation use in agency program management and policy making. Similarly, Congress can play a decisive role in fostering results-oriented cultures in the federal government by using information on agency goals and asking for and using financial and performance information as it carries out its various responsibilities.

Chairman Issa, Ranking Member Cummings, and Members of the Committee, this concludes my prepared statement. I would be pleased to respond to any questions that you may have at this time.

GAO Contacts

For further information regarding this testimony, please contact Robert F. Dacey, Chief Accountant, at (202) 512-3406 or daceyr@gao.gov; Gary T. Engel, Director, Financial Management and Assurance, at (202) 512-3406 or engelg@gao.gov; or J. Christopher Mihm, Managing Director, Strategic Issues, at (202) 512-6806 or mihmj@gao.gov. Contact points for our Offices of Congressional Relations and Public Affairs may be found on the last page of this statement.

Appendix I: Chief Financial Officers (CFO) Act Agencies: Fiscal Year 2012 Audit Results and Principal Auditors

CFO Act agency	Opinion on the agency's financial statements	Agency had a noncompliance issue[a]	Principal auditor
Agency for International Development	[b]	√	Office of Inspector General (OIG)
Agriculture	Unqualified	√	OIG
Commerce	Unqualified	√	KPMG LLP
Defense	Disclaimer	√	OIG
Education	Unqualified	√	Ernst & Young LLP
Energy	Unqualified		KPMG LLP
Environmental Protection Agency	Unqualified	√	OIG
General Services Administration	Unqualified	√	KPMG LLP
Health and Human Services	[c]	√	Ernst & Young LLP
Homeland Security	[d]	√	KPMG LLP
Housing and Urban Development	Unqualified	√	OIG
Interior	Unqualified	√	KPMG LLP
Justice	Unqualified		KPMG LLP
Labor	Unqualified		KPMG LLP
National Aeronautics and Space Administration	Unqualified		PricewaterhouseCoopers LLP
National Science Foundation	Unqualified		CliftonLarsonAllen LLP
Nuclear Regulatory Commission	Unqualified		CliftonLarsonAllen LLP
Office of Personnel Management	Unqualified		KPMG LLP
Small Business Administration	Unqualified	√	KPMG LLP
Social Security Administration	Unqualified	√	Grant Thornton LLP
State	Unqualified	√	Kearney & Company
Transportation	Unqualified	√	KPMG LLP
Treasury	Unqualified	√	KPMG LLP
Veterans Affairs	Unqualified	√	CliftonLarsonAllen LLP

Source: GAO.

[a] Reported noncompliance with applicable laws and regulations and/or substantial noncompliance with one or more of the Federal Financial Management Improvement Act requirements.

[b] The auditors of the U.S. Agency for International Development's (AID) fiscal year 2012 financial statements issued a qualified opinion because of the effects of a number of unsupported adjustments on AID's financial statements.

[c] The auditors expressed an unqualified opinion on the Department of Health and Human Services' fiscal year 2012 accrual-based financial statements, but were unable to express opinions on the department's 2012 Statement of Social Insurance and 2012 Statement of Changes in Social Insurance Amounts.

[d] The auditors of the Department of Homeland Security's (DHS) fiscal year 2012 financial statements issued a qualified opinion because of DHS's inability to provide sufficient evidence to support certain components of property, plant, and equipment and heritage and stewardship assets presented in the financial statements and notes.

GAO's Mission	The Government Accountability Office, the audit, evaluation, and investigative arm of Congress, exists to support Congress in meeting its constitutional responsibilities and to help improve the performance and accountability of the federal government for the American people. GAO examines the use of public funds; evaluates federal programs and policies; and provides analyses, recommendations, and other assistance to help Congress make informed oversight, policy, and funding decisions. GAO's commitment to good government is reflected in its core values of accountability, integrity, and reliability.
Obtaining Copies of GAO Reports and Testimony	The fastest and easiest way to obtain copies of GAO documents at no cost is through GAO's website (http://www.gao.gov). Each weekday afternoon, GAO posts on its website newly released reports, testimony, and correspondence. To have GAO e-mail you a list of newly posted products, go to http://www.gao.gov and select "E-mail Updates."
Order by Phone	The price of each GAO publication reflects GAO's actual cost of production and distribution and depends on the number of pages in the publication and whether the publication is printed in color or black and white. Pricing and ordering information is posted on GAO's website, http://www.gao.gov/ordering.htm. Place orders by calling (202) 512-6000, toll free (866) 801-7077, or TDD (202) 512-2537. Orders may be paid for using American Express, Discover Card, MasterCard, Visa, check, or money order. Call for additional information.
Connect with GAO	Connect with GAO on Facebook, Flickr, Twitter, and YouTube. Subscribe to our RSS Feeds or E-mail Updates. Listen to our Podcasts. Visit GAO on the web at www.gao.gov.
To Report Fraud, Waste, and Abuse in Federal Programs	Contact: Website: http://www.gao.gov/fraudnet/fraudnet.htm E-mail: fraudnet@gao.gov Automated answering system: (800) 424-5454 or (202) 512-7470
Congressional Relations	Katherine Siggerud, Managing Director, siggerudk@gao.gov, (202) 512-4400, U.S. Government Accountability Office, 441 G Street NW, Room 7125, Washington, DC 20548
Public Affairs	Chuck Young, Managing Director, youngc1@gao.gov, (202) 512-4800 U.S. Government Accountability Office, 441 G Street NW, Room 7149 Washington, DC 20548

www.ingramcontent.com/pod-product-compliance
Lightning Source LLC
Chambersburg PA
CBHW080758290526
45790CB00008B/3502